First World War
and Army of Occupation
War Diary
France, Belgium and Germany

3 DIVISION
8 Infantry Brigade
Gordon Highlanders
4th Battalion
11 March 1915 - 29 February 1916

WO95/1421/2

The Naval & Military Press Ltd
www.nmarchive.com
Published in association with The National Archives

Published by

The Naval & Military Press Ltd

Unit 10 Ridgewood Industrial Park,

Uckfield, East Sussex,

TN22 5QE England

Tel: +44 (0) 1825 749494

www.naval-military-press.com

www.nmarchive.com

This diary has been reprinted in facsimile from the original. Any imperfections are inevitably reproduced and the quality may fall short of modern type and cartographic standards.

© **Crown Copyright**
Images reproduced by permission of The National Archives, London, England, 2015.

Contents

Document type	Place/Title	Date From	Date To
Heading	WO95/1421/2 3 Divn 8 Inf Brig 4 Bn Gordon Highlanders 1915 Feb-1916 Feb		
War Diary	L.A. Clytte	11/03/1915	31/03/1915
War Diary	Vlamertinghe	01/06/1915	20/06/1915
War Diary	Hooge	19/07/1915	23/07/1915
War Diary	Dickiebusche	01/08/1915	31/08/1915
Miscellaneous	In The Field		
War Diary	Sanctuary Wood	17/09/1915	18/09/1915
War Diary	Bivouack 3/4 Male E of Ouderdom	19/09/1915	23/09/1915
War Diary	Sanctuary Wood	24/09/1915	25/09/1915
War Diary	Rest Bivouac 3/4 M.E Of Ouderdom	26/09/1915	30/09/1915
War Diary	Eecke	02/11/1915	20/11/1915
War Diary	Reninghelst	21/11/1915	09/12/1915
War Diary	Dug Outs	15/12/1915	31/12/1915
Heading	1/4 Gordon Hrs Jan Vol XI 3rd Div 76th Inf Bde		
War Diary	Dugout	01/01/1916	05/01/1916
War Diary	Mervieux	29/02/1916	29/02/1916

WO 95 1421/2
2 DIVD.
8 INF BRIG
4 BN. GORDON HIGHLANDERS
1915 FEB - 1916 FEB

Instructions regarding War Diaries and Intelligence Summaries are contained in F. S. Regs., Part II. and the Staff Manual respectively. Title pages will be prepared in manuscript.

INTELLIGENCE SUMMARY.

or

(Erase heading not required.)

Place	Date	Hour	Summary of Events and Information	Remarks and references to Appendices
LA CLYTTE	11th Decr		Batt. still in Huts. D coy in trenches 1 man killed	
"	12th "		B coy went into the trenches with 1st Gordon Highrs. 2 men wounded	
"	13th "		Officers of C coy reconnoitred G 3 & 4 trenches. B coy with 1st Gordons 1 man wounded	
"	14th "		Ordered to take over trenches G 3 & 4, H 1 with two Coys. remainder to take up billets in LOCRE. C & D coys paraded for trenches but whole move cancelled on account of German attack on ST ELOI. C D Coys Officers reconnoitred H 1.2.3.& 4 trenches 1 man wounded	
"	15 " "		Inspection of Transport & B Gs. A Coy came out of the trenches	
"	16 " "		Battalion took over G 3 & 4. H 1.2.3 & 4 trenches with C & D coys. A coy in support. B coy regained from trenches with 1st Batt in reserve at ROSSIGNAL	A/7/5
"	17 " "		Batt. held G 3 & 4. H 1.2.3.& 4 trenches changed that night to K 2 & BEC with C coy & 2 M.G. D coy in reserve. A & B coys back to LA CLYTTE. 2 men wounded C coy 1 man killed D coy	
"	18 " "		C coys still in trenches D coy in reserve. Officers of A & B reconnoitred new trenches	
"	19th "		C coy relieved by D coy 2 men killed and one wounded C coy. A & B coy took over new part of line had quarters attached to 1st Gordons in VIERSTRAAT. B coy in the trenches 2 men killed one man wounded	
"	20th "		A & B in 'N' trenches C & D in K2 trenches. 1 man casualties A & B	
"	21st "			
"	22d "		.... 1 man killed one wounded	
"	23d "			
"	24th "		A & B in 'N' trenches C & D coys relieved in K2 trenches by the East Surreys. returning to Huts at LA CLYTTE 1 man killed	

1577 Wt. W10791/1773 500,000 1/15 D. D. & L. A.D.S.S./Forms/C. 2118.

INTELLIGENCE SUMMARY

(Erase heading not required.)

Place	Date	Hour	Summary of Events and Information	Remarks and references to Appendices
LA CLYTTE	25th March		"B" Coy relieved A Coy in Trenches C & D in huts at LA CLYTTE	
"	26th		A & B Coys came out of N Trenches being relieved by 1st Gordon Hghrs and rejoined rest of Batt. in huts	
"	27th		Battalion in huts at LA CLYTTE	
"	28th			
"	29th		C & D Coy relieved B Coy 1st Gordons in ⅚ N Trenches also 2 Trenches from 2nd Royal Scots	
"	30th		C & D Coys in N & M 5 Trenches	
"	31st		C & D Coys in N & M 3 Trenches	1/73

Samuel Lock Copinal
Lt Gordon Hghrs

INTELLIGENCE SUMMARY.

(Erase heading not required.)

Place	Date	Hour	Summary of Events and Information	Remarks and references to Appendices
VLAMERTINGHE	1-6-15		"C" and "D" Coys in fire trenches. "A" and "B" relieve "C" and "D" Coys at night. 1 Killed and 1 wounded.	
"	2-6-15		"A" and "B" Coys in fire trenches. "C" and "D" Coys in reserve. Very heavy bombardment on HOOGE. 1st Gordons and our trenches. Casualties however comparatively slight, only 11 men being wounded by shrapnel. All quiet except one German made two infantry attacks last night on trenches in neighbourhood of HOOGE, but both were driven back by the Cavalry.	
"	3-6-15		"A" and "B" Coys in fire trenches. "C" and "D" Coys in support. Very quiet today. 2 wounded.	
"	4-6-15		"A" and "B" Coys in fire trenches. "C" and "D" Coys relieve "A" and "B" Coys at night. Some heavy shelling in the evening. One officer wounded (2/Lt Simpson)	
"	5-6-15		"C" and "D" Coys in fire trenches. "A" and "B" Coys in reserve. Quiet Day	
"	6-6-15		"C" and "D" Coys in fire trenches. "A" and "B" Coys in reserve. Quiet Day. One man wounded.	
"	7-6-15		"C" and "D" Coys in fire trenches. "A" and "B" relieve "C" and "D" at night. 2/Lieut. Hodkinson and 4 men wounded.	
"	8-6-15		"A" and "B" Coys in fire trenches. "C" and "D" in reserve. Quiet Day. 2 men wounded.	

Place	Date	Hour	Summary of Events and Information	Remarks and references to Appendices
HEBUTERNE / LANCERTINQUE	16/6/15	2 a.m.	Dawn broke on a very quiet morning. There was considerable mist. Our Artillery Bombardment commenced on the 'Y' wood at 2.50 am. The ranging was very accurate. The bombardment almost ceased for 15 minutes between 3.30 am & 3.45 am then it commenced again. The mist had to some extent cleared, but fumes still thick, in the hollows this, combined with the great amount of smoke, made observation very difficult.	
		4 a.m.	Bombardment heavier and fairly accurate. It ceased at 4.15 am. The 7th Brigade then advanced to the attack. They had little difficulty in capturing the 1st line German trenches. Very little could be seen of its advance.	
		7-10am	Fairly quiet. The Germans were firing a few shells, mostly shrapnel. Verbal orders from Brigadier General, afterwards confirmed to push the company to the 'Y' wood with orders. They were to reoccupy a portion of German trench captured in the morning. At 10.30 'D' Coy. advanced to 'Y' wood, undergoing heavy shelling from shrapnel. No men could be found in Y wood, & all the trenches being occupied by our men and our men coming [?] back, being driven back by the men [?] stopped & reached Germ line in Y wood.	
		11 am		
		12 am	'D' Coy Hqs themselves in to Y wood having failed to discover any trench. On reaching by our men, orders of any means of working them was considerable confusion, & no orders could	

INTELLIGENCE SUMMARY.
(Erase heading not required.)

Place	Date	Hour	Summary of Events and Information	Remarks and references to Appendices
VLAMERTINGHE	16/6/15	12am	could be got 9 any out.	
		1pm	Heavy German bombardment of Y. Wood lasting for 2 hr, the shelling continued during the afternoon and evening. All trenches were severely shelled.	
		2pm	Shelling slackens slightly, message received from Brigade that 42nd Brigade support attack, and attain original objective. Turn to be ordered later.	
		3pm	42nd Brigade arrive in our front line trenches, but are unable to advance further, because of heavy German shell fire. They also suffered from German "GAS" shells. One Batt. crowded into our fire trench. Trenches behind Y. Wood, wooded with a view to having two Companies then in support ? D Coy. Shed trench were however found very much congested with 42nd Brigade, and no more coy. could	
		5pm	German shelling very fierce for 1 hr., especially at Y. Wood.	
		6pm	the 42nd Brigade with does to Ypres.	
		7pm	Shelling slackens considerably. Farm nearby 9th Sqn. shelled. Bill recommend German gas shells.	

INTELLIGENCE SUMMARY.

(Erase heading not required.)

Place	Date	Hour	Summary of Events and Information	Remarks and references to Appendices
VLAMERTINGHE	16.6.15	6 p.m.	Quiet	
		6 p.m.	A few shrapnel and S.A. shells falling.	
		10 p.m. to 12 midnight	Collection of wounded &c. Received orders that the Batt. was to go to Brigade reserve at G.H.Q. line. 'D' Coy relieved in Y wood at midnight. Casualties: Majr E. A. Smith, Lieut D.S.P. Drayton, 2/Lt J.A. Clarke, and 2/Lt J.D. Pratt all wounded.	
	17.6.15		Whole Battalion in G.H.Q. line in Reserve. 7 men killed, 46 wounded, 1 missing. Shots Battn found Lieut J.A. Clarke, and 2/Lt J.D. Pratt all wounded. Battn. furnished working party to Engineers. the Germans shelled the communication trench for first time. 3 killed 5 wounded.	
	18.6.15.		A & D Coys in G.H.Q. line, remnants of 'C' Coy in support trench 23. 'C' Coy North of road to Menin Road, B Coy North of road, 'C' Coy go to Y wood, to bury dead. Quiet day. No casualties.	
	19.6.15.		Batt. in trenches as for 18th. Some shelling during the day. Were relieved by the K.R.R. about 9.30 p.m. & marched back to bivouacs behind VLAMERTINGHE. 1 man killed 6 wounded.	
	20.6.15		In rest at bivouacs. 1 man accidentally wounded.	

WAR DIARY or INTELLIGENCE SUMMARY

Army Form C. 2118.

Instructions regarding War Diaries and Intelligence Summaries are contained in F. S. Regs., Part II. and the Staff Manual respectively. Title pages will be prepared in manuscript.

Place	Date	Hour	Summary of Events and Information	Remarks and references to Appendices
HOOGE	19/7/15	8 P.M.	German artillery very active for about an hour	
		9 P.M.	German artillery fire much slacker	
		9.30 P.M.	Orders received to send one Coy to return to 2nd Coy 4th Middlesex Regt at ISLAND POINT. A Coy started from Dug outs at 10.30 P.M. along with 8 bombers who reinforced the 4th Middlesex in the mine crater	
		11. P.M.	Much quieter. Casualties 4 killed 13 wounded include 2/Lt SPRATT wounded	
	20/7/15	1 A.M.	Orders received to send all available bombs to OC 4th Middlesex Regt	
		3 A.M.	Orders received to send all bombers to report to 4th Middlesex at ISLAND POST. One Officer and 12 bombers left at 4.30 A.M.	
		4 A.M.	A Coy returned leaving the B bombers under D/Lt Allardyce in communication trenches forward from the crater.	
			During the day Germans shelled us heavily and with increased force from 6 to 8 P.M.	
		8 P.M.	Orders received as to disposition in case of German counter attack. 2 Suffolk Regt came up in reserve.	
			Our bombers were employed in German trenches forward from crater	
		11.30 P.M.	German shell fire slackened Casualties 3 killed 18 wounded	
	21/7/15		Fairly quiet day a few German shells & trench mortar bombs. Bombing squad relieved by fresh squad about 5 P.M. Casualties 1 killed	
	22/7/15		Very quiet day. Bombers returned from crater at 3.30 P.M. Casualties 2 killed 1 wounded. Batt relieved at night by 8th K.R.R. returning to Bivouack at BRANDHOEK	
	23/7/15		In Bivouack at BRANDHOEK Orders received to take over trenches 31 & 32 from 14th Bde on night of 24th.	

WAR DIARY or INTELLIGENCE SUMMARY

Army Form C. 2118.

(Erase heading not required.)

Instructions regarding War Diaries and Intelligence Summaries are contained in F. S. Regs., Part II. and the Staff Manual respectively. Title pages will be prepared in manuscript.

Place	Date	Hour	Summary of Events and Information	Remarks and references to Appendices
DICHIEBUSCHE	1.8.15		In bivouack one mile N. of DICKIEBUSCHE	
"	2.8.15		In bivouack. C2 Coys on digging fatigue during day, diggers trench for telephone wires. 4 men wounded by shrapnel. 1 man sick. Lieut. R.A. HUGHES. M.O. sick.	
"	3.8.15		Battalion took over L 28, 29, 30 & 31 Support trenches from 1st Gordon High[rs]. Capt Seterkin in command of Battalion. Major Lyon on leave. Capt ackd. Mac Intosh sick. Transfers on lorries YPRES – COMMINES canal.	
"	4.8.15		3 men sick. & Rgt. C.R.BRANDER. Battalion in trenches. 4 men sick	
"	5.8.15		Battalion in trenches one man killed. 1 man accidentally wounded. 1 man sick	
"	6.8.15		Battalion in trenches one man wounded. Draft of 73 men arrived at not bivouades	
"	7.8.15		Battalion in trenches one man wounded. 1 man accidentally wounded. 4 men sick	
"	8.8.15		Battalion in trenches Major Lyon returned from leave and took over command that night. two 1 man sick 3 men wounded	
"	9.8.15		Battalion in trenches. As 6th Div. was attacking at HOOGE Battalion was ordered to try & create a diversion, by grenade and rifle fire. Trenches shelled intermittently by enemy. 1 man killed 2 wounded	
"	10.8.15		Battalion in trenches. Some shells & one of our trenches & high explosive shrapnel D.H. Road F.A. killed 2 men killed, nine wounded. Battalion relieved by 1st Gordon High[rs] D Coy. left at BEDFORD house as Brigade reserve	
"	11.8.15		Battalion in rest billets one mile N. of DICKIEBUSCHE Capt. J.H. Beggs sick	
"	12.8.15		" " " " " " " 1 man sick	
"	13.8.15		" " " " " " " 3 man sick	
"	14.8.15		" " " " " " " A & B Coys. worked at fortified farm at	
"	15.8.15		Joint Sheet 28 H 16 D 22	
"	16.8.15		Battalion in rest billets one mile N. of DICKIEBUSCHE 2 men sick	

INTELLIGENCE SUMMARY.

(Erase heading not required.)

Instructions regarding War Diaries and Intelligence Summaries are contained in F.S. Regs., Part II. and the Staff Manual respectively. Title pages will be prepared in manuscript.

Place	Date	Hour	Summary of Events and Information	Remarks and references to Appendices
DICKIEBUSCHE	17/8/15		Battalion in rest billets south N. of DICKIEBUSCHE. 2 men sick.	
	18/8/15		" " " " " " 3 men sick	
	19/8/15		" " " " " " 3 men sick	
	20/8/15		" " " " " " 1 man sick	
	21/8/15		" " " " " "	
	22/8/15		" " " " " " 2 men sick	
	23/8/15		" " " " " " Draft of 59 men arrived	
	24/8/15		" " " B.L.C. Coys to wood collecting fascines in YPRES. 1 man sick	
	25/8/15		" " " A&D Coys digging telephone cable in near ZILLEBEKE Lake. 1 man sick	
	26/8/15		" " " A.B&C Coys working at practical from abt 28 HD11. 1 man sick	
	27/8/15		" " " " " " 1 man sick	
	28/8/15		" " " " " " Brigade sports. 1 man sick	
	29/8/15		" " " " " " 1 man sick	
	30/8/15		" " " " " " 1 man sick	
	31/8/15		" " " " " "	

Aug 31st 1915

S.P. McClintock Capt acting
Lt. Gordon Highrs.

1577 Wt.W10791/1773 500,000 1/15 D.D.&L. A.D.S.S./Form/C.2118.

Place _____
Date _____

To be rendered in accordance with Field Service Regulations, Part II.

FIGHTING STRENGTH

This should *not* include details attached to unit, or personnel detailed to march with the Train, or any men unfit to go into action with unit

RATION STRENGTH

To include Fighting Strength, Personnel detailed to march with the Train, and all Personnel and animals attached for Rations and Forage

UNIT	Personnel		Horses and Mules			Other Animals	Guns and Ammunition Wagons (stating nature)	Machine Guns	Ambulances	Tool Carts, Technical Carts (stating nature)	Remarks	Personnel	Horses and Mules		Other Animals	Mechanically Propelled Vehicles					Remarks
	Officers	Other Ranks	Riding	Draught and Pack								Total, all Ranks entitled to Rations	Heavy Horses with R.G.A.	Other Horses and Mules		Motor Cars	Motor Bicycles	Lorries 3 Ton	Lorries 30 Cwt.	Tractors	
(1)	(2)	(3)	(4)	(5)	(6)	(7)	(8)	(9)	(10)	(11)	(12)	(13)	(14)	(15)	(16)	(17)	(18)	(19)	(20)	(21)	(22)	(23)
	21	534	11	26	31	8	4 Lewis	4	—	17				11	2	8	17	26	1	8		
	22	534	11	2	8	21	4 Lewis	4	—	17		23 552	11	3	3	17	26	1	8		
	21	604	10	2	5	5	7 Lewis	4	—	17		24 559	10	3	5		26	1			
	23	584	21			2	8 Lewis	4	—	17		23 631									
	25	56			16	2	8 Lewis	4	—	17		27 593	19	16	2	26	8				
	21	631	19	15	2	26	8 Lewis	4	—	17		29 656	19	15	10	26	8				

TOTALS ....

Ammunition with Unit :—
- .303 inch; approximate number of rounds per Man _____
- .303 inch; " " " per Machine Gun _____
- Gun or Howitzer; approximate number of rounds per Gun or Howitzer _____

Supplies with Unit :—
Approximate number of days' rations for men of ration strength _____
" " " forage for Animals " _____
" " " fuel and lubricants for Mechanically Propelled Vehicles _____

Signature of Commander _____

Forms B. 231

WAR DIARY of 4th Gordon H[ighlanders]
or
INTELLIGENCE SUMMARY

Army Form C. 2118.

Instructions regarding War Diaries and Intelligence Summaries are contained in F. S. Regs., Part II. and the Staff Manual respectively. Title pages will be prepared in manuscript.

(Erase heading not required.)

Place	Date	Hour	Summary of Events and Information	Remarks and references to Appendices
SANCTUARY WOOD	17/9/15		Fine day. Usual activity. Our guns @ 9.5 rectified by day as well as night. This was the first time this was held & they never been drawn out about 6 weeks ago. Germans at various times day & night tried to get up to it about then communication trench but always stood in some our fire at them on our throw 2 or 3 bombs. This seemed our shut when tried to come up. CT	
	18/9/15		Fine day. Heavy bombardment began at 6:30am on N of MENIN road for about an hour. Enemy replied but not on our trenches. Our guns bombarded Fort & Foundry in afternoon about 2 PM. Enemy replied, but some Whiz bangs came over our trenches. Trenches were cleared. Relieved by 1st Line Regt but our usual working parties instead of to 12 midnight, so as at to leave a dr Staff marched back to hut billets about half E of OUDERDOM. 2 men wounded while away on dug out party. (Mackey) (2 men sick)	
Bivouack 3 mile E of OUDERDOM	19/9/15		Fine not billets, huts Foster & Cranston left out in trench area to night on condition of enemies trenches & wire etc & any change in addition made. Fine	
	20/9/15		In hut billets. Fine (1 man sick)	
	21/9/15		In hut billets but up and pioneers all night to trenches to make dug outs for officers, water carts, wash tubs with material for same. Very good reports received daily from L/Sgt Foster 2 men sick	

WAR DIARY or INTELLIGENCE SUMMARY

Army Form C. 2118.

(Erase heading not required.)

Instructions regarding War Diaries and Intelligence Summaries are contained in F. S. Regs., Part II. and the Staff Manual respectively. Title pages will be prepared in manuscript.

Place	Date	Hour	Summary of Events and Information	Remarks and references to Appendices
3rd Bn E Y R OUDERDOM	22.9.15		So met General Field Marshal Lord Kitchener inspected 3rd G.H., 1st G.H., 2nd R.S. & 3rd Canadian Bdes afterwards & said that G.H.Q. had done excellent work so far & he was sure it would do the same in the events which were to take place in the next few days. Bn warned for the trenches tomorrow night. First 3 order sent.	
"	23.9.15		Battalion left for the trenches, strength marching out 27 Officers & 614 other ranks. Took over trenches C1. B8. C15. D.g.s. C1R & R.S1 all in SANCTUARY WOOD from 1/ Lincoln Regt.	
SANCTUARY WOOD	24.9.15		In trenches in SANCTUARY WOOD, busy getting everything ready for attack. Copy of operation orders attached.	
"	25.9.15	1.30 am	A small ration of coffee distributed in Dixies to men; immediately afterwards all ranks moved into their assaulting positions; everyone in their correct positions by 3.40 am.	
		3.50 am	Our bombardment commenced; almost at once Germans started bombarding our trenches, mostly with Crumps, some casualties mostly in C.15 and Half moon street.	
		4.50 am	Our bombardment lifted off German front line trenches.	
		4.10 am	½ of B coy crawled forward towards German line	
		4.15 am	½ of D coy & ½ of C coy advanced & the other half advanced from our second line trenches.	

WAR DIARY 4th Gordons
or
INTELLIGENCE SUMMARY.

(Erase heading not required.)

Army Form C. 2118.

Place	Date	Hour	Summary of Events and Information	Remarks and references to Appendices
			been captured thus. Sergt Forbes was killed about this point by a shell. Lieut Henderson now in command of C Coy (Capt Reid having been wounded in the middle of the redoubt & carried back to our own lines by his servant) reported that he was at point J.13.c.79. with 6 men he was afterwards driven back from this by shell fire.	
		4.50 pm to 12 noon	Heavy shelling from Germans all the time. Reinforcements were asked for 2 Coys in German 3rd line and half of B Coy under Capt Watson were sent up. Capt Watson was wounded in afterwards by a shell.	
		5 pm –5.30 pm	One Half A Coy in reserve in B.S.S. was sent for to take the place of B Coy in C1 as supports. All our old trenches were being heavily shelled by Whiz bangs which made it very difficult to get up supplies of bombs etc even as far as the redoubt, but it was done all night and a bomb reserve was made in German front line at point J.13.c.3-9. but it was found almost impossible to take them further forward than there.	
		About 11–12 am	Germans collected in half of German road & at about 11.30 am – 12 noon attacked from N & N.E. with bombs, parties up the trenches and b others over the open. Our bombers with some of the 1st G.H. who were isolated from their own battalion	

Army Form C. 2118.

WAR DIARY 4th A. Cyclist Regt.
or
INTELLIGENCE SUMMARY.
(Erase heading not required.)

Instructions regarding War Diaries and Intelligence Summaries are contained in F. S. Regs., Part II. and the Staff Manual respectively. Title pages will be prepared in manuscript.

Place	Date	Hour	Summary of Events and Information	Remarks and references to Appendices
Rest Bivouac 2 m. E. of OUDERDOM	26/9/15		Battalion rested. Church parade at 6.p.m. in evening.	
"	27/9/15		Corps Commander Lt. Gen. Sir E.H.H. ALLENBY K.C.B. came and addressed the battalion, explaining situation & complimenting the battalion on what they had done. (5 men sick to F. Amb)	
"	28/9/15		Divisional Commander Lt. Gen. J.A.L. HALDANE came & addressed the battalion, explaining situation & the necessity of continuing attacks & complimented the battalion on the way they had attacked.	
"	29/9/15		[illegible]	
	30/9/15	5.p.m.	Orders received direct from 3rd Div. with 8 ordinary ordnance battalion to be to move as soon as possible and to march to Bivy outs in H.23.B near KRUISSTRAAT	
		8.30 pm	Arrived there at 8.30 p.m.	
		9.30 pm	Got a message from 3rd Div. to supply a party of 150 men to carry bombs from KRUISSTRAAT to MAPLE Copse. 2nd Batt. officer with fatigue load of bombs & had to use the whole of the battalion to carry them to MAPLE copse. Total strength out about 300. Very heavy work as men in marching order & very wet underfoot. Carrying parties sent off in small parties of 10 & arrived at MAPLE copse about 2 a.m. 3 men wounded & shell fire on the way.	

WAR DIARY or INTELLIGENCE SUMMARY.

Army Form C. 2118

(Erase heading not required.)

Instructions regarding War Diaries and Intelligence Summaries are contained in F. S. Regs., Part II. and the Staff Manual respectively. Title pages will be prepared in manuscript.

Place	Date	Hour	Summary of Events and Information	Remarks and references to Appendices
EECKE	2/11/15		Still in Rest Billets. Draft of 50 men arrived including 4 injured & 2 men admitted hospital. New draft inspected by C.O. 1 man admitted hospital.	
	3/11/15		do Usual parade	
	4/11/15		do Quantity of ammunition carried on men reduced to 120 rounds. 1 man to Hospital	
	5/11/15		do Final of Divisional Football Competition at STEENVOORDE. Arrangements made for a Batt. Boxing Tournament. 2689 L/Sgt Bridges awarded the "Croix de Guerre".	
	6/11/15		do Communion Service. Between 50 men joined the Church Kit - and equipment inspection by C.O. 2 men to Hospital	
	7/11/15		do men instructed in use of Iron helmets. Battalion practical blocking trenches	
	8/11/15		do Practical "Outposts"	
	9/11/15		do Batt. route march. Batt. supplied working party to construct Parapets, rifle range. Instructor Jacqueron leaves to be attached to 8th Bde. Sgt. Burns returned to England pending Commission	
	10/11/15		do 3 men arrived including 2 rejoined	
	11/11/15		do Practical building parapit and blocking C.T.S. No 1 Coy practical shooting on Rifle range	
	12/11/15		do Usual parade. Football matches played in afternoon	

WAR DIARY
or
INTELLIGENCE SUMMARY.
(Erase heading not required.)

Army Form C. 2118.

Place	Date	Hour	Summary of Events and Information	Remarks and references to Appendices
EECKE	13/11/15		Still in rest Billets. Practice in building parapets, blocking trenches, and drainage. Sinus material used.	
	14/11/15		do. Church parade in School Playground. Inspection of billets by C.O. A draft of 50 men arrived, including 4 rejoined.	
	15/11/15		do. New draft inspected by C.O. Usual parades - No 2 Coy drilled in afternoon wearing late recruits. First arrivals.	
	16/11/15		do. Boxing (light-weight) wrestling pillow fighting. 1 man to Hospital. The recent draft put under Capt. Bowcher for training. Parades as usual. Trials of Battalion Sports.	
	17/11/15		do. Battalion route march. Afternoon devoted to football. Major A. Lyon returned from instruction at 8 Bde. H.2. and took over duties of Adjutant. 6 men arrived including 1 rejoined.	
	18/11/15		do. Kit-inspection of A & B Coys by the Brigadier-General who also inspected the transport. He expressed himself pleased with both. Fatigue parties sent to H.2 Tent Riding R.E. to make galvans and new pattern travel. Six officers proceeded by motor bus to attend exhibition of Aeroplane photos at RENINGHELST. The journey each way lasted 1½ hours. The exhibition 25 minutes. Party very disappointed. 1 man to Hospital. Weather very cold wet.	

1577 Wt.W:o791/1773 500,000 1/15 D.D. & L. A.D.S.S./Forms/C. 2118.

Army Form C. 2118

WAR DIARY
or
INTELLIGENCE SUMMARY.
(Erase heading not required.)

Instructions regarding War Diaries and Intelligence Summaries are contained in F. S. Regs., Part II. and the Staff Manual respectively. Title pages will be prepared in manuscript.

Place	Date	Hour	Summary of Events and Information	Remarks and references to Appendices
EECKE	19/9/15		Still in rest Billets. Battalion warned to proceed on 20th to trench area with a view to occupying position as Reserve and Pioneer Batt on night 21/22. Filled in all practice trenches, weather very frosty and much colder.	
	20/9/15		Battalion marched to Rest Billets at RENINGHELST. marched at 10 am and arrived at 2 pm weather fine and frosty glad to march for 2 hours in a field with 8 East SURREYS defaulted. Dinners were taken during the march Specialists conveyed from EECKE to RENINGHELST by motor busses arrived at 10 pm. a portion of these was to proceed to a portion of these at 2.30 am to take over from 2 London Regt. Rest Camp Consisted of tents and a few huts. Ground fairly dry ground of mud Specialists left at 2.30 am to take over Church Parade 10 Evr in turn. Battalion paraded for trenches at 2.40 pm. A Coy + 25% Specialists still in Camp	
Reninghelst	21/9/15		Battalion marched at 3 pm to trench area and relieved 3rd London Regiment. Buy at on Canal in area of Bluff (C33.a.4.5) R + L. Relief completed 7.59 pm. No casualties Night was clear and very frosty. Details at Camp ordered to leave for Smith Hop Given two days to move 1 man to Fd. Amb.	

WAR DIARY
or
INTELLIGENCE SUMMARY.

(Erase heading not required.)

Army Form C. 2118

Place	Date	Hour	Summary of Events and Information	Remarks and references to Appendices
Reninghelst	22.		Quiet day. Very frosty, men worked all day improving dug outs, and surrounding up to field ambulance. Provided fatigue for moving material, no casualties. 1 man to Details. Site for new camp G.35.c.3.2. chosen & marked out. Drew 25 tents from Ordnance and erected camp, with French troops as working party.	
	23		Movedto new Camp and busy whole day on improvements. Started etc. Officers mess, latrines etc. Pte Beggs sentence of 9 mths hard labour by Court martial was promulgated today before details. Very quiet day in trench area. Frosty in morning but mild rain at night - work of reconstructing dug outs continues slowly as ground everywhere is in very bad state. 1 man wounded. My bullet while on ration fatigue. 13 men to Fd. Amb.	
	24		Details go on sick parade, chiefly colds. Carried on work in Camp. Men all busy keen on getting things into order. R E Park have been of great assistance in supplying us with wood for building purposes. In trench area things very quiet in our section but considerable shelling all day to our north. Our Snipers shot one German from the BLUFF and harassed several working parties. Our Snipers have taken over the "Shooting on the BLUFF" from the R.W. FUSILIERS, weather dull with some rain. Continued work on dug outs and on supporting points. 1 man to Fd. Amb.	

Army Form C. 2118.

WAR DIARY
or
INTELLIGENCE SUMMARY.
(Erase heading not required.)

Instructions regarding War Diaries and Intelligence Summaries are contained in F. S. Regs., Part II. and the Staff Manual respectively. Title pages will be prepared in manuscript.

Place	Date	Hour	Summary of Events and Information	Remarks and references to Appendices
RENINGHELST	25.11.15		"A" Coy relieved "B" Coy in the dug outs. Commenced new line of emplacement in GORDON POST also making loopholed dugout in R.10. Continued improving dug-outs. 1 man to Fd. Amb.	
	26.11.15		Continued work as above. Dug-outs now in much better condition. LANKHOF CHATEAU bombarded for about 3 minutes by 15 cm guns apparently trying to find a battery of ours. 1 man to Fd. Amb.	
	27.11.15		MAJOR SMITH and other Officers relieved C.O. and Officers in trench area. Very quiet day. 2 men to Fd. Amb.	
	28.11.15		Very cold frosty all day. Work in dug-outs, R.10, R.11 carried on as usual. 2 men to Fd. Amb.	
	29.11.15		Our H.A.R. registered on trenches opposite 33 & 35. Otherwise quiet. Carry improvement continues but hindered by lack of wood. 1 man to Fd. Amb.	
	30.11.15		German trenches opposite 34 & 36 bombarded with field guns & howitzers. Results appear to have been satisfactory. Last day of work in dug-outs as we are moved to commence work on repairing C.T.'s. 3 men to Fd. Amb.	

Alexander Lyon Major
O/C of Gordon Hrs.

WAR DIARY or INTELLIGENCE SUMMARY

Army Form C. 2118.

Place	Date	Hour	Summary of Events and Information	Remarks and references to Appendices
RENINGHELST	1.12.15		Weather fine. Quiet but active in evening. Heavy firing to the South which sounded as if in vicinity of KEMMEL. Commenced with repairing C.T.'s but work rather held up through shortage of material. 1 man to Fd. Amb.	
	2.12.15		Weather fine, work continued on dugouts & C.T.s. One gun rather active. 1 N.C.O. wounded by shrapnel in C.T. 33 left. 4 men to Fd. Amb.	
	3.12.15		"C" Coy relieved "D" Coy in dug outs. Officers' relief also carried out. Work in C.T.s continues.	
	4.12.15		Weather misty and raining. H.A.R. fires at enemy's snow chaps. with good results. A sheet of flame was seen to rise up after the burst. Of one shell. Japan out-enemy trooper trench located & registered on by a fresh gun placed at Pt. Bann (Intelligence Officer) disposal. Arrangements made to send over some shrapnel during night. Work as usual. Capt. Bran du arr. ret. fr. Rouen to relieve Lt. Mc Mass appointed to S.D. wounded staff. 1 Officer & 40 men East Yorks attached to Bde for work, accommodated in our dug. out area. Carried on with canals improvements.	

WAR DIARY or INTELLIGENCE SUMMARY

Army Form C. 2118

Place	Date	Hour	Summary of Events and Information	Remarks and references to Appendices
Reninghelst	5/12/15		Ježek French burial still in morning. Snipers saw working party and dispersed them by shell fire. German shot by sniper in a trench at Tower of Hollebeke station fell down in the afternoon. Guns annoyed at short time on both sides. The Dump inside H.Q. Dug anti aeroplanes at about 5 p.m all bursting fairly high. None as usual. Maxim Rennan relief. Suffered as were in position from us on South Side of Canal. Men in Camp Church Parade in Y.M.C.A. Hut, Inspection of kit. of the men returned from the Trenches.	
	6/12/15		Fine day, a good deal of shelling in the direction of Brigade Headquarters in the evening (otherwise quiet)	
	7/12/15		Fairly dry today - truth the exception of a few shells which landed in the rear of dugouts stopped Infantry Quiet. Around Dear Tree walks knew, considerable amount of small shells dropped	
	8/12/15		Cold - this morning Alfred - 10 a.m - a carrier & no. 16 Amular of shells dropped around Dealer Fytn and one man (probably a civil) severely wounded in right leg by H.E. Shrapnel. He was lost in the charge, Majd[?] Syn Left Lens (Segan) (wounded) for the 8th Brigade. One man (military?) Killed at the entrance to Dear Tree walks about 2p.m by (a whiz bang	
	9/12/15		Heavy shelling early this morning over on right. Very little of about 11 am and continued to Null of continued strong wind the day	

WAR DIARY
or
INTELLIGENCE SUMMARY.

(Erase heading not required.)

Army Form C. 2118.

Instructions regarding War Diaries and Intelligence Summaries are contained in F. S. Regs., Part II. and the Staff Manual respectively. Title pages will be prepared in manuscript.

Place	Date	Hour	Summary of Events and Information	Remarks and references to Appendices
Dug outs	15/10/15		Heavy enemy bombardment. Heavy shelling cause[d] blas[t] in the trench and our artillery retaliated.	
	16/10/15		Weather very nicely. Enemy shelled a good deal recent[ly]. Sec. Lieut. Ison Major Lory appointed to Lieut. Dormant Suffering from Lancaster Regt.	
	17/10/15		Very quiet today and hardly any shelling at all.	
	18/10/15		Quiet day. Draft of 250 men arrived in Camp today	
	19/10/15		Heavy rifle fire early this morning. Direct down a strong bomb of the farm north and heavy bombardment from trench old city and from our heavy artillery. German bombarded trench on railway	
	20/10/15		Shelling heavy again today. Most intermittent with rifle discharge bombardment. Fifteen killed on the morning near light railway on road.	
	21/10/15		Dull quiet and very little shelling.	
	22/10/15		Dry where in the morning commenced to rain about 1 noon. Some shelling in the vicinity of theatre during the afternoon.	
	23/10/15		Dull cloudy, hardly any shelling at all.	
	24/10/15		Heavy rain over night, but dry and clear in the morning. Almost an entire absence of any shelling.	

Army Form C. 2118.

WAR DIARY
or
INTELLIGENCE SUMMARY.
(Erase heading not required.)

Instructions regarding War Diaries and Intelligence Summaries are contained in F. S. Regs., Part II. and the Staff Manual respectively. Title pages will be prepared in manuscript.

Place	Date	Hour	Summary of Events and Information	Remarks and references to Appendices
Dug Out	25/10/15		Very clear this morning and apparently no shelling wherever throughout the day.	
	26/10/15		Clear bright this morning. No shelling in the forenoon but in the course of the afternoon the enemy sent over quite a few shells close to the right of Supply Trench. Had a gas alarm sounded at 11.30 pm.	
	27/10/15		Raining overnight but clear and bright in the morning. Fair quiet all day.	
	28/10/15		Quiet all day.	
	29/10/15		Quiet early part of day, but a good deal of shelling in afternoon.	
	30/10/15		Clear & bright this morning even with shelling. Dry bright hardly any shelling during the day. At 11 pm some heavy shelling by our artillery without eliciting any reply from the enemy.	

John H. Cleverson Lt.
of Regiment 2nd Bn
4 Gordon Highlrs.

1/4 Gordon Hrs
Jan
Vol. XI

3rd R.M
76mm Ber
70. 8" 13en 2.2.16.

Army Form C. 2118.

WAR DIARY
or
INTELLIGENCE SUMMARY.
(Erase heading not required.)

Instructions regarding War Diaries and Intelligence Summaries are contained in F. S. Regs., Part II. and the Staff Manual respectively. Title pages will be prepared in manuscript.

Place	Date	Hour	Summary of Events and Information	Remarks and references to Appendices
			[Page rotated 90°; handwriting largely illegible. Partial readings:] Very quiet in morning, but enemy after noon kept up a steady rifle fire and burst shrapnel on our left from Laventie onwards. Very quiet in the evening but commenced to fire about midnight. A good deal of shelling by the enemy in the afternoon of Rutoire Farm & Richebourg.	
	4/11/15		Very clear this morning. Report from enemy quiet but shells into Laventie châteaux. Heavy firing through day till about midnight. Then from the French — severe fire came from...	
	5/11/15		Dull morning. Very quiet morning. Our heavies were firing most of forenoon at Aubers Church. The enemy shelled our front line trenches. Canal banks. Very heavy fire. Very clear this morning. Very quiet. Enemy sent over a few shells near Brigade HQ Mont Bernenchon; in the evening till about 11 o'clock shelling about 100yds in front of our HQ trenches.	

1577 Wt. W10791/1773 500,000 1/15 D. D. & L.   A.D.S.S./Forms/C. 2118.

WAR DIARY
or
INTELLIGENCE SUMMARY

(Erase heading not required.)

Place	Date	Hour	Summary of Events and Information	Remarks and references to Appendices
MERVIEUX	29.2.16		to MERVIEUX where we billeted month in trains. had march on men carrying out a bright but mild setting.	
	1/3/16			Spencloth afficds 1/4 Gordon Highrs

www.ingramcontent.com/pod-product-compliance
Lightning Source LLC
Chambersburg PA
CBHW081504160426
43193CB00014B/2588